The Depth of a Woman

Norhan Ahmed

BookLeaf Publishing
India | USA | UK

The Depth of a Woman © 2022 Norhan Ahmed

All rights reserved.

No part of this publication may be reproduced, stored in a retrieval system, or transmitted, in any form or by any means, electronic, mechanical, photocopying, recording or otherwise, without the prior written permission of the presenters.

Norhan Ahmed asserts the moral right to be identified as author of this work.

Presentation by *BookLeaf Publishing*

Web: www.bookleafpub.com

E-mail: info@bookleafpub.com

ISBN : 9789357446297

First edition 2022

DEDICATION

I dedicate this to my grandmother – your love, faith, and strength carry me through each day of my life.

ACKNOWLEDGEMENT

To all the encouraging, kind human beings that have come and gone from my life that have supported me, read my work, and pushed me to continue despite any hesitation. I honor each and every one of you that has come my way. Your words and actions have an everlasting impact. Thank you.

PREFACE

Why I Write-

It is natural for human beings to retreat inward and isolate themselves when they are alone. I have felt alone many times in my life. Writing has always been the go to medium for solace and expression.

I share my pain for those who suffer like me in the dark. I do it for the ashamed, depressed, and defeated. All these I have felt. Once read, written words are absorbed by the mind. They can either be food or poison. At its core, writing is healing. When I pick up my pen and paper, I think of myself and others. This is my motivation. To share than to release.

The Girl With Raven Hair

Long ago there was a girl with raven hair
she was light
she was warmth
she lit any room she walked into

As the years passed,
her light dimmed
Unfortunate circumstances and people met her

Her radiance turned into a low light
She absorbed what she should have observed
The peace within her turned into chaos
Her optimism turned into negativity

Her happiness turned into anger and despair
Dark days followed
Chaos consumed her within
Outwardly she was still smiling, still kind, still
caring,
but the chaos would not waver
As soon as any negative emotion reached it
it was fueled and strong
it was the unlovable part of her
when buried it would rise to the surface
the chaos was the strength of ten fires
It was not put out easily by her prayers

The turning point came when she realized she
wasn't alone
We have all been tainted by our unfortunate
circumstances
We all have chaos within us
In different forms and colors

The young woman looks back at the younger
version of herself
And says
I will return to you one day
Carefree and vibrant as I once was
I will turn this chaos that has caused weakness
to step into my power
I will make you proud

A Young Arab Woman

From young
We were raised on the belief that marriage was
sacred
Ingrained within us
A milestone we need to achieve

When we reach a certain age
Unconsciously we begin to chase that ring

It is hard to cultivate healthy relationships with
our men
Their own mothers wrecked with misogyny and
contempt
Teaching their sons to control
To oppress and manipulate their wife

The "open-minded" of them are indeed lost
Putting on a facade
The close-minded are evil

When I speak about this
I am told I am generalizing
But I want to scream at the top of my lungs
That so many women have suffered
So many are suffering

Abandonment

I do not cry over any endings in my life anymore
Not friends who have disappointed me
Not potential lovers who whispered sweet words
in my ear
And eventually left

I know that I can not keep anything that leaves
Even if I have it between my teeth
It will still find its exit

Every chapter has a season
And I need to maintain my peace

D.A.B

Your sweet compassionate soul came into my
life at a time when I needed you. I was drowning
under the crashing waves of my own pain. I
needed your spirit

My heart always skipped a beat when I saw your
name anywhere

I know no one is perfect but— she is lucky to
have you by her side

Having a crush on someone is an easy way for
us to swallow the fact that we actually love them

An "I like you" is easier to move on from than
an "I love you"

I don't see much of a difference, maybe it's just
something we have convinced ourselves of to
avoid the true pain of loss in love

I knew it was love when— I'd rather have you
for a few months or a few years than never
experience your love at all
Nothing I do will make you mine so I hide my
true feelings behind friendship

Empowered

A year ago, around the summertime, I remember I was kneeled over on the cold cold floor. So much pain. You called yourself a pioneer of mental health. Where was your consideration for mine? This pain brought to my awareness wounds I was not conscious of. Hurt on top of hurt. A downward spiral followed.

I was only a woman who wanted to love you. To know you. Yet, you vilified my love and turned it dark. Tainted it with your insecurities and self-loathing. For months, I went back and forth between regret, anger, and sadness. Your name would be mentioned in conversations unprovoked, and it would feel like a shooting pain in my heart.

After some time, we reconnected briefly. I thought I had healed. I thought I was okay. But God made sure you would hurt me again once more. One night, I turned to God in prayer, and He whispered to me "Never go back to what broke you. Broken people break others"

Safety

I have never felt safe in the arms of a man. I
never felt stable, peaceful, nor comforted. Not
by the men who raised me. Not even in the arms
of the man I had my child with. I have never felt
the intimacy of being secure in the presence of a
man who was supposed to love me.

Every time I let my guard down thinking I found
the one I can be myself with, I get stung. How
long will this keep repeating?

I am scared I won't recognize a healthy love
when it comes. I am scared I will doubt a
genuine person's intentions. I do not want to
punish a good man for another cowardly man's
actions.

She

She rose with the sun
Slept with the moon
An ethereal being
full of curiosity and light
Full of love
Too much love in a world that makes it
feel like a sin

Memories

9

I can miss you and still
know that your chapter in my story
is over

Healing

Untying all these small knots inside me
Letting the pain be realized
Setting it free
Allowing space for healing to happen

Allowing it to breathe
Not judging myself for feeling a certain way
Not judging my feelings toward situations and
people

I have never felt like I belonged anywhere
Not the place I was born
Nor my family's country of origin
I always felt I was meant to deposit
Pieces of my soul around
I was meant to travel and discover the crevices
and corners
Of the world no one knew

11/11

Maybe I was meant to love you from a distance
I see your name everywhere
On a poster
On a flyer
Every syllable and letter pieced together
Your name is common

I will never get the chance to be a part of your
life
To know you the way I want to
To be close to you
And feel skin on skin
It is so cruel to have these feelings
These dreams

And never be able to turn to you and say
"These feelings I expressed a year ago
still call my heart it's home
But now I must make them unalive"
It must all end

Strength

On the days
When my strength fails me
And my head is deep in my hands
In despair
May I always be reminded of my inner
resilience
And how much I have overcome
Both good and bad times have a purpose

Pen to paper

There are times I want to write
My hand suddenly becomes stiff
Words I am afraid to write
Fearful to read over

Memories I want to suffocate
People I want to unknow
Entire chapters I wish to rip from my book

To burn
Remembering
Nothing can be undone

There is no undo button in life
I bring my pen to the paper once more
There is no other way but to write
This is all I have known

Past-Life Connection

Intense
A supercharged connection fueled with
emotions that spans several lifetimes
Souls with a knowing
Moving through the motions of time
Foreign yet familiar

A soul contract that has the power
to heal
to hurt
to put one on the right path

The timing precarious
meant to meet
not meant to last

A Child of the Diaspora

Where is home?
Is it our parent's place of origin
In the streets of Cairo
Arabic spoken on the tongue
Or is it our place of birth
In the bustling vibrant city of the west?

Is it where we have established residence
Or where we have traveled to seek better
opportunity

Is it the years we have spent building a life in
one place
Or the ancestral blood running through our veins

Inside we are torn
Never fitting completely
In either world

A tug of war happens
When we travel back
We are both and neither
Split in half
The product of the diaspora

Grief

The grief I feel over your passing
It is as if those eight years were eight days
On repeat
The sadness is fresh
As if I am stuck in the moments when I realized
we lost you
A nightmare on constant replay
Grief is a feeling that is always there
But its intensity comes and goes
It can strike at its strongest at any hour or place
I plead with my tears
I am not always in safe company
I wonder who taught us to label our grief as
inappropriate
As if it is the worst thing in the world to cry

Dear K

The first man in my life
From you
I have known unconditional love
You held me up
In the early years of my life

Married at the age of 17
To the love of your life
Created a life together

Thirty-five years of a blissful union
Children that brought grandchildren
Now that your grandchildren have grown up
You have become unrecognizable

Unconditional love came from you
But you taught me that anything good can turn

I was introduced to a different kind of loss
The loss of a loved one while they are still alive
The pain of looking into your face not
recognizing the
man who raised me

The day you left
You broke your partner's heart

And broke mine

I cried tears alongside her
Did you know she died from a broken heart?

At times I have to fight with myself not to
taint my childhood memories
With the terrible memories
you will leave me with

All that loss and love
Has called upon me
To find forgiveness
Allow it to envelope my heart

I am not there yet
But I will be

11:11

To the man I will meet:

Anything I require I can reciprocate in tenfold
Anything I lack
I will allow you to teach me
There will be parts of you that you claim are
unlovable and can't be changed
I promise to love and accept those parts of
you
On the days when the balance tips over and
you need affection
I promise to show up for you
And fill your half-filled cup and make it full

When you allow me the safe space to be my true
self
I won't hide the parts of me I was asked to
hide

But promise me that we will not get lost in each
other
That we will remain our own separate person
With our own individual goals and purpose
United at the center of our hearts

I promise to share with you all the reasons that

made me who I am
And my troubles
If you promise to share yours
Secrets keep two people disconnected
And honesty is an act of love
I want to know what the man in front of me is
made of
What has bitten him and tainted him
What affects him

On the days when fruit tastes in our
mouth sour
I will sprinkle the sweetness of love in
whatever you taste

When the nights turn extra dark
Promise
To hold me tighter as I fight off fears and
nightmares that hold residence in my mind

Promise me we won't ever raise our voices in a
fit of anger
Anger is such futile emotion
It is fleeting yet destructive
That our fight against whatever it may be is a
collective one
Against something
Not against each other

Promise me that you understand that we will
have bad days
Sometimes at the same time
When our mental well-being takes a
dive
Promise me that we will swim together in this
cold ocean only holding on to each other

Promise me that the injustices of this world will
never stop to cause you the anger it rightfully
deserves
Let us share in this anger and make a
difference together
Let us build and form communities that others
will find comfort in
Let us create something together that will live
longer then we will

Let us leave a legacy behind that will have our
children say my parents changed lives
Let us live this short life with purpose
In adventure and spontaneity
In true love and sacrifice
In service of others

Let our souls be one of giving more than taking
Let us not absorb the bitter taste of greed
Or feel the fires of jealousy

The day I meet you
The moment we connect
Is the day we plant this seed
A garden will grow from this one seed
This connection is eternal
Continuing even after we have both expired